THIS PAMPHLET IS TO BE
INCLUDED IN THE EMERGENCY
PACKS OF AIRCRAFT OPERATING
OVER THE DESERT

DESERT

SURVIVAL

A.M. PAMPHLET 225

PENGUIN BOOKS

PENGUIN BOOKS

UK | USA | Canada | Ireland | Australia
India | New Zealand | South Africa

Penguin Books is part of the Penguin Random House group of companies
whose addresses can be found at global.penguinrandomhouse.com.

First published by the Air Ministry 1952
First published in Penguin Books 2017
001

The moral right of the author has been asserted

Printed in Great Britain by Clays Ltd, St Ives plc

A CIP catalogue record for this book is available from the British Library

ISBN: 978–1–405–93167–0

www.greenpenguin.co.uk

DESERT

SURVIVAL

DESERT SURVIVAL

INTRODUCTION

1. The word "desert" invariably produces in one's mind a picture of large, dry, barren tracts of land, hot in the daytime and cool at night, where the problem of survival is one of the first magnitude.

2. When it is realized that there is at least one desert in each continent of the world, it will be appreciated that this problem of survival is a very real one in the lives of those who fly. Approximately one-fifth of the world's land area is composed of desert, while the population of these areas amounts to less than one-twentieth of the total world population.

3. The aim of this pamphlet is to provide you with the necessary information to enable you to survive if you have to make a forced landing or parachute descent in the desert. You are urged to read it and thoroughly acquaint yourself with its contents, especially if you are operating over such terrain—it may save your life.

PRINCIPAL DESERTS OF THE WORLD

4. There are more than fifty important deserts in the world, the areas of which range from 300 to 3,000,000 square miles. The larger of these are well-known: Sahara (3,000,000 sq. mls.); Libyan (650,000 sq. mls.); Arabian (500,000 sq. mls.); Gobi, Mongolia (400,000 sq. mls.); Rub al Khali, part of the Arabian Desert (250,000 sq. mls.); and the Kalahari, Bechuanaland (200,000 sq. mls.).

5. The deserts with the most extreme climates are: the Sahara of North Africa; the Middle-Eastern deserts of Arabia, Iran and Iraq; parts of the Gobi in Mongolia; and the narrow strip along the coasts of Peru and Northern Chile. The Great Sandy Desert in Western Australia (160,000 sq. mls.), and the Mohave of the Southwestern United States and Northern Mexico (13,500 sq. mls.), are not "extreme" deserts, but they contain large waterless tracts which can present serious survival problems to aircrew.

DESERT CHARACTERISTICS

6. All deserts have certain things in common. Scarcity of water and great extremes of temperature are the outstanding characteristics. Rainfall is scarce though in parts of the Middle East it may be heavy during the winter. Surface water is absent over great areas for months at a time. Desert areas are generally cloudless, and high winds prevail over the larger ones for much of the year, with resulting serious sand and dust problems. Plant, animal, and human life is sparse and concentrated near the water sources. These oases, with their date groves and garden patches, may support up to 1,000 people per square mile. Large parts of the deserts however, are practically lifeless for long periods.

Surface Conditions

7. Deserts have various surfaces. Only a small part of them consists of soft sand (the popular conception of a desert). About a tenth of the Sahara is sandy, the greater part being a flat, barren, gravel plain from which the wind has blown the sand away and piled it up in the low-lying areas where the dunes are to be found. There are also mountainous areas, such as comprise the perimeter of the Arabian peninsular, varying in height from 6,000 to 12,000 feet. Other types of surface are plains dotted with sparse grass and thorny bushes (as in the Kalahari), mud flats and lava flows. There are lakes in some deserts, but permanent desert lakes with no outlets are salt lakes.

Climate

8. The temperature range in the extreme desert regions is considerable—hot days may be followed by freezing nights, the temperature dropping by as much as 50 to 70 degrees Fahrenheit. The following examples will serve to illustrate this point. At Habbaniya, in Iraq, the maximum and minimum temperatures recorded during the month of July are 123 deg. F. and 60 deg. F. respectively, while in January maximum and minimum recordings are 79 deg. F. and 16 deg. F., thus giving an annual variation of 107 deg. F. In the Western Sahara, the annual variation is very similar, ranging from a maximum of 125 deg. F. to a minimum of 22 deg. F. Sun temperatures during the hot season

often exceed these figures and have been known to reach 180 deg. F. The coldest desert is the Gobi, where the yearly absolute range is from 110 deg. F. in the summer to −40 deg. F and even −50 deg. F. in the winter, although the daily variation in temperature is less than that of the Sahara, being 25 deg. F. to 35 deg. F.

9. The following table is extracted from the meteorological data available at Habbaniya over a period of 14 years, and may be taken as typical of the Middle-Eastern deserts:—

RAINFALL AND TEMPERATURE RECORDS—HABBANIYA

1935-1949

	RAINFALL				TEMPERATURE			
	Mean Rainfall	Highest M'thly	Lowest M'thly	Highest in 24 hrs.	Mean Maximum	Mean Minimum	Highest	Lowest
	mm.	mm.	mm.	mm.	°F.	°F.	°F.	°F.
JANUARY	21.2	60.2	Trace	30.5	60.3	39.1	79	16
FEBRUARY	15.8	32.3	0.6	20.6	65.1	42.0	87	24
MARCH	24.1	83.1	0.1	28.5	75.0	47.9	97	27
APRIL	8.4	20.2	Trace	13.2	85.3	57.3	106	38
MAY	2.6	14.5	Trace	9.2	98.2	67.8	116	50
JUNE	Nil	Trace	Nil	Trace	106.7	73.2	120	60
JULY	Nil	Trace	Nil	Trace	111.6	77.9	123	69
AUGUST	Nil	Trace	Nil	Trace	111.7	76.7	122	67
SEPTEMBER	0.1	0.5	Nil	0.5	104.4	69.5	119	52
OCTOBER	2.5	20.8	Nil	15.2	92.4	61.3	107	42
NOVEMBER	17.6	39.8	Trace	24.3	76.4	51.0	95	33
DECEMBER	22.7	77.5	Trace	28.2	63.1	41.9	79	20

10. A thorough knowledge of the conditions likely to be encountered by a crew following an emergency descent into the desert, and adequate preparations at base are essential for survival. Before each flight, carefully check all emergency equipment in the aircraft, and personal survival equipment, and ensure that all items are serviceable. Immediately replace any that are missing or have deteriorated (see A.P. 1182C, Vol. 1 for scale of equipment). Remember that WATER is the first essential—your life depends on your water supply in the desert, so carry all the water you possibly can. If you have more equipment than you can carry, sacrifice anything but water. If the weight allowance of your aircraft is small (10 lbs. or less) put all of it into water. Only if you feel that you are carrying enough water, and if you have weight allowance left, should you pack food, emergency equipment, etc. The standard contents of the emergency packs may be modified to suit individual needs and local conditions. This should not be done on your own initiative, however, as it is dangerous with certain types of packs, such as those fitted in ejection seats.

11. The following items, in addition to water, should be carried if possible: heliograph, signal pistol and cartridges or flares, a small reliable compass, maps (indicating roads and sources of water if possible), tinted flying goggles or sun glasses, head covering, knife, matches, salt tablets, a minimum of concentrated emergency rations, first aid kit, anti-burn cream, torch, warm clothing (for use at night), and a pair of strong boots. A useful maxim to bear in mind is "always fly in the boots in which you intend walking home".

12. Your parachute is invaluable as an item of survival equipment in the desert. The canopy will give you shelter from the heat of the sun during the day and protection against cold at night. The pack itself can be modified to provide a knapsack, while the shroud lines will be found useful for many purposes.

13. Remember that if you are compelled to bale out, much of the equipment stowed in the aircraft will be lost to you. Make a point of carrying on your person some of the smaller items,

particularly a heliograph and signal flares. Failure to do this may jeopardize your chances of survival.

14. Make sure that you thoroughly know the emergency signals procedure and the rescue facilities available in the area over which you intend to fly. Proper use of these facilities will enable the rescue co-ordination centre to initiate search action promptly and limit the area of uncertainty.

15. Learn all you possibly can about the conditions you are likely to encounter in your particular area. Find out about the inhabitants, whether they are friendly or not, their customs, etc. Make a point of talking to crews who have had personal experience of desert survival—they will probably be able to give you some useful hints, and you may profit by their mistakes.

ACTION IN AN EMERGENCY

16. The captain of the aircraft should take immediate signals action if there is any danger, or possibility of danger, so that the ground station may be informed of the situation. These messages can always be cancelled if the emergency passes, but if omitted the aircraft may disappear without trace, making search action and subsequent rescue considerably more difficult.

17. When it becomes impossible or inadvisable to continue the flight two courses of action are open to you—a forced landing or a parachute descent. Over the desert a forced landing is preferable, as not only will the aircraft provide you with shelter and many items of emergency equipment, but will be a conspicuous landmark for searching aircraft. So try and stay with the aircraft and bring it down if possible. If the emergency is caused by lack of fuel, you should attempt a landing while you still have enough power to locate a suitable area and carry out the approach and subsequent crash landing.

18. In certain areas the prevailing wind direction can be determined by the formation of sand dunes which usually run approximately at right angles to it. These "sand seas" should be avoided if possible and a landing made on level ground, but if this is not feasible, and you have the choice of landing into wind or parallel

to the dunes, land across wind and parallel to the dunes. Avoid salt pans and wadis. Bear in mind the task of your rescuers, who may have to reach you by land rescue teams, and try to keep clear of areas which are impassable to them. Always try to bring your aircraft down near water sources or well-defined tracks, so that your chances of survival and rescue may be increased. A surface wind of any strength will be indicated by blowing dust. Landings should be made with the undercarriage retracted, even though the surface of the area chosen appears to be level and free from obstructions; it may be too soft to support the wheels, resulting in the aircraft turning over onto its back. If the aircraft has a fixed undercarriage, or the undercarriage cannot be retracted, do not use brakes during the landing run unless to avoid obstacles.

19. If you are forced to bale out, observe the descent of the aircraft and make your way to the wreckage if it is within reasonable distance. Even a wrecked aircraft is conspicuous from the air and will yield useful emergency equipment, so use it as a rendezvous for your crew.

IMMEDIATE ACTIONS AFTER LANDING

20. Leave the aircraft as soon as it has come to rest, taking with you as much water as you can and, if possible, your parachute and emergency packs. Stay well away from the aircraft until all danger of fire has passed.

21. There will be a great temptation to rush around trying to do everything at once. Try to resist this. *Take it easy.* Get into the shade immediately. Weigh up the situation calmly and decide on your course of action. There will be two things requiring your immediate attention—first aid and shelter.

First Aid

22. Attend promptly to all injuries. Remove all injured personnel into the shade as soon as possible. Follow the established first-aid practices:—

(a) *Wounds.* See that open wounds are dressed to prevent infection by dust and sand. Cut away clothing and don't handle the wound. Keep the wounded part at rest.

(b) *Fractures.* Fractured limbs should be immobilized by splints improvised from tight rolls of clothing or parts of the aircraft. (A hacksaw will be found useful for this purpose.) Don't remove clothing from the limb, but cut it away from wounds and dress them before splinting.

(c) *Hæmorrhage.* Control severe bleeding by applying a tourniquet between the injury and the heart. Release the tourniquet for half a minute every fifteen to twenty minutes.

(d) *Shock and Internal Injury.* Should be treated by keeping the person lying down and warm. If conscious, a hot drink can be given, provided the injury is not abdominal.

(e) *Sprains.* Bandage the injured part and keep it at rest until it can be moved without great pain. If swelling increases, remove the bandage to relieve the pressure and then rebind.

(f) *Burns.* Don't open blisters. Use the anti-burn cream in the first-aid kit or make a saline solution with the salt tablets and apply a dressing soaked in the solution to the affected part. Don't change the bandage, and keep the burned part at rest.

(g) *Cessation of Breathing.* If an injured man has stopped breathing, pull his tongue forward and apply artificial respiration. Check for head injuries or fractured skull (indicated by unequal pupils or bleeding from the ears or into the skin around the eyes.) Be very careful in handling such patients.

Shelter

23. Natural shelter will be limited to the shade of cliffs or hills. During most of the year the inside of the aircraft will be unsuitable as a shelter in the daytime owing to the intense heat. Even at night in the summer, in some deserts, it will be untenable. Only during the winter months should it be used for this purpose.

24. If the erection of a permanent shelter calls for exertions that will increase the sweat rate, this should be delayed until the temperature has dropped sufficiently to enable the work to be undertaken in comfort and, if necessary, a temporary shelter should be rigged to provide shade in the meantime.

25. The best shelter from the sun is provided by the wing of the aircraft. If the aircraft is resting firmly on the ground, with no danger of movement in a strong wind, the most suitable shelter can be improvised by draping a parachute canopy from the trailing edge of the mainplane. The lower edge of the canopy

DOUBLE LAYER OF PARACHUTE DRAPED OVER AIRCRAFT WING PROVIDES GOOD SHADE

should be not less than two feet from the ground to allow the air to circulate freely, and both upper and lower edges should be firmly secured. To reduce heat and glare most effectively, two parachute layers should be used, allowing an air space in between.

26. If the aircraft is a low-wing type, and resting on soft sand, scoop away the sand from under the mainplane to increase the clearance. By doing so you will dig down to where the sand is several degrees cooler. In most deserts, at a depth of 30 inches the temperature is below 70° F.

27. Other types of shelter can be made from your parachute, dinghy apron, tarpaulins, or blankets, using sticks, rocks, or removable parts of the aircraft for supports. Always use a double layer of material for added protection, and allow an air space round the bottom which can be closed at night for warmth. Such shelters must be firmly secured against the prevailing high winds. Beds should be raised off the ground for greater cooling effect.

28. The aircraft will afford shelter from the cold during winter nights, when the temperature may drop to freezing or below, and from the violent rainstorms which may occur in most deserts at some season. Failing this, your parachute again will be invaluable in providing you with shelter. Erect it in the form of a bell tent, pegging the sides to the ground or using rocks to keep them down. In the rainy season, camp on high ground and dig a drainage trench round the base of your shelter, with a "lead-away" trench running down the slope to prevent an accumulation of water. Collect this water to supplement your water supply.

PARACHUTE SHELTER FOR COLD WEATHER

PLAN OF ACTION

29. As soon as possible after landing and attending to immediate personal needs, the situation should be carefully sized up and a plan of action decided after discussion between all crew members. This must be done at the outset, when you are sufficiently fresh mentally and physically to think clearly. Once you have made your decision, stick to it, even though it may later appear to be wrong—your capacity to reason will diminish as time passes.

30. Decision must be reached on the following items, and perhaps others, peculiar to a particular emergency:—

    (a) Decision to stay or travel.

    (b) Rationing of water and food.

    (c) Signals contact.

(d) Ground signals.

(e) Allocation of duties.

(f) Log keeping.

(g) Preparation of landing strip or dropping zone.

Decision to Stay or Travel

31. Whether to stay or travel is the most important item for consideration. On it largely depends your chances of survival. The decision rests with the captain of the aircraft and must be based on a careful estimate of the situation. Factors which will influence the decision are:—

(a) *Position.* Try to pinpoint your position by studying maps, landmarks, flight log, or even by astro. You must know where you are before you can decide intelligently whether or not to remain with the aircraft, and to plan your direction and duration of travel if you do decide to walk out. If you were on track, or if your position is along a recognized air or land route, your chances of rescue from your present position are good.

(b) *Radio Contact.* Were you able to establish radio contact and transmit a distress message before making your forced landing or baling out? Can you contact ground stations or other aircraft from your present position?

(c) *Equipment.* Prepare an inventory of your emergency equipment, removing all items that are likely to be adversely affected by heat from the inside of the aircraft and storing them in the shade. Decide whether you have enough water and food for a desert trek and the chances of replenishing your supplies en route. Travel requires more water and food than staying in the shade. Reference to the water table on page 21 will show you how far you can expect to travel on the water available. What items can be improvised from parts of the aircraft? Is your clothing and footwear adequate for walking?

(d) *Physical Condition.* Consider your physical condition and that of the other members of the crew and estimate your ability to endure travel. Are you capable of carrying the equipment you require for a trek? Remember that a gallon of water weighs 10 lbs. If any of the crew are injured you may have to send the two strongest men for help. Don't send one man alone if it can be avoided.

(*e*) ***Weather.*** Does the prevailing weather allow adequate visibility for search action?

32. The best advice is to stay with the aircraft for at least five days—your chances of rescue are greatest during this period. The advantages of this action are:—

(*a*) The aircraft is easier to locate from the air than persons travelling.

(*b*) The aircraft provides you with shelter, signalling aids, and other useful emergency equipment.

(*c*) You will avoid the difficulties and hazards of desert travel.

33. Experience has shown that most rescues have been made when crews have remained with their aircraft.

Before you make a decision, consider ALL the factors.

Rationing of Water and Food

34. Rationing of water and food should be instituted immediately. It is impossible to lay down any hard and fast rules about rationing, as the amount of the daily ration will depend on several factors: the quantity available, your position, the probable lapse of time before rescue, and the chances of replenishing your supply (largely dependent on the season of the year).

35. The minimum daily water requirement to maintain life in the desert is a variable quantity, depending on the range in temperature, the physical condition of the person, and the degree to which he can protect himself from exposure to sun and heat.

36. Study paras. 59 to 77 on water consumption and the accompanying water tables, so that you can determine your bodily

water requirements and relate them to the existing conditions. Conserve your supply by keeping it in the shade to avoid evaporation and refrain from smoking, especially during the heat of the day.

37. If your emergency pack contains one of the plastic drinking cups, the ration may be measured by reference to the ridged divisions, each of which represents approximately two fluid ounces (20 Fluid Ounces=1 Pint). The tins of water contain 14 fluid ounces, or approximately two-thirds of a pint.

38. When drinking, the lips, mouth, and throat should be moistened before swallowing.

39. Food is of secondary importance to water and the quantity taken should be very much restricted in hot climates if the amount of your daily water ration is less than one pint. A man in good condition can live for long periods without food, if he has sufficient water. If the daily water ration is less than one quart, don't eat foods rich in fat which require a considerable amount of water for their digestion and for the elimination of waste products. The best foods to eat are those of the carbohydrate, or sugar and starch group, such as potatoes, fruits, and the sweets in the emergency flying rations, which require very little water for their digestion. Vary the quantity of food according to the amount of water available; if the water ration has to be decreased, the food ration must be decreased in proportion.

40. When you are located by search aircraft, do not assume that rescue is imminent and consume all your supplies. If the first contact is made at night the position obtained by the aircraft may be only approximate, and a further day search may be necessary to establish it with greater accuracy before the dispatch of rescue teams. It may be some time before these rescue parties can reach you, so continue with strict rationing until you are picked up.

41. All ration issues should be recorded in the log at the time of issue so as to avoid arguments later.

Signals Contact

42. The aircraft radio is your best rescue aid. Although its range on the ground will be considerably reduced, this can be improved by erecting a vertical aerial—it is more efficient than the horizontal aircraft aerial. If the set is serviceable, transmit an S.O.S. message as soon as possible, giving your position, if known. Intersperse your transmission with 20-second dashes to allow D/F stations to take your bearing, and always conclude with the time at which you propose to transmit again. Always listen out before transmitting to ensure that the frequency is reasonably clear. If no reply is received, switch off and call again at fixed intervals. Always conserve your batteries—transmissions should be kept as short as possible—and make certain that all other electrical circuits (lights, gunsights, etc.) are switched off. Batteries may, if necessary, be topped up by urinating in them. If there is no risk of fire through fractured pipelines, etc., run up the engine charging the generator during transmission and reception, if possible—you will get better signals and lengthen the life of your batteries. This will require sufficient R.P.M. to bring in the cut-out so that the generator takes over the load. It should also be remembered that ground running of engines in the desert quickly leads to overheating and engine temperatures must be carefully watched. Engines should be kept covered when not in use to prevent entry of sand and dust. Transmissions at night on the appropriate destress frequency will give you greater range and, owing to the drop in temperature, will not cause the engine to overheat so quickly.

43. When using the Radio Transmitter SCR 578 ("Gibson Girl") in the desert, bury the ground contact and wet it with urine to increase the sending range, otherwise the range will be only a few miles. Under ideal conditions during the rainy season in the desert the range should be about 50 miles. If the weather is not suitable for using the kite, the aerial should be payed out to its fullest length and attached to the highest part of the aircraft.

44. The transmitter should be operated for periods of 4 minutes, at intervals of about 10 minutes, but if a serviceable and accurate watch is available you should transmit for periods of at least 3 minutes starting at 15 and 45 minutes past each hour.

45. With the radio set to automatic transmission, signals take the following form:—

Auto 1 Position—S.O.S. for 20 seconds followed by a continuous dash for 20 seconds.

Auto 2 Position—S.O.S. for 20 seconds followed by 4-second dashes for 20 seconds.

46. As the Auto 2 Position is designed to operate the automatic alarm on surface vessels, transmissions in desert regions should normally be confined to the Auto 1 Position, unless it is estimated that the crash position is such that transmissions on the Auto 2 Position may be received by surface craft (e.g. along the coastal strip of North Africa). In such case the 4-minute period should consist of 2 minutes on the Auto 1 Position followed by 2 minutes on the Auto 2 Position.

47. If the crash position is known, this can be transmitted along with any other information on the Manual Position outside the above periods.

48. The Radio Transmitter T3180 ("Walter") should be used sparingly. The life of the battery will be drastically reduced in tropical conditions and in extreme cases may fall to eight hours or even less. As a general rule, "Walter" should be used only when it is known that aircraft are in the vicinity. If a single aircraft has made a forced landing in the desert, it is pointless to switch on "Walter" immediately unless the aircraft is on a recognized route frequented by other aircraft. Better to conserve "Walter's" life until other aircraft have been able to start search action.

49. The transmitter should be switched on for periods of 2 minutes at 5-minute intervals, and should be left switched on if aircraft are heard or are known to be in the vicinity.

Ground Signals

50. Try to make your position as conspicuous as possible from the air. Full use should be made of equipment and materials whose colours form a contrast with the natural surroundings. Signalling equipment should be ready for use immediately an aircraft is heard—delay may be fatal. The following are some of the more practical methods of attracting attention:—

(*a*) Engine cowlings, removed and placed upside down make good reflectors, also portions of a metal wing surface from which the camouflage has been scraped. Surfaces can be brightly polished with sand or gravel—the reflection will be very apparent from the air in daylight.

(*b*) Spread out the dinghies and parachutes if they are not needed for shade.

(*c*) Use the heliograph for signalling during the daytime. This is the most effective visual signalling method when the sun is shining, ranges of 20 miles having been achieved. Rear vision mirrors or polished food tins will also serve this purpose. Signalling by these means should be practised regularly so that there is no delay in focusing when an aircraft is sighted.

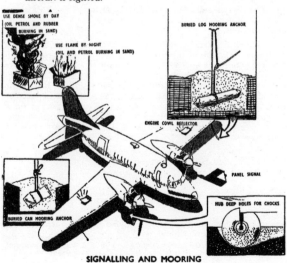

SIGNALLING AND MOORING

(*d*) Ground strips should be prominently displayed in the form of the signals given in the Ground/Air Emergency Code. In some areas it will be found possible to prepare signals by removing the top-soil and exposing the contrasting sub-soil.

(*e*) By night, if the landing lights are still intact, remove them from their housings and arrange them so that the

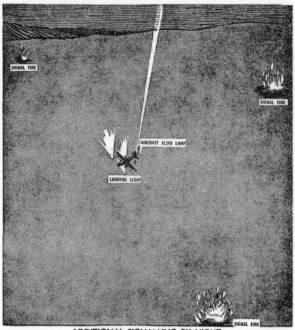

ADDITIONAL SIGNALLING BY NIGHT

reflectors are free to be pointed in all directions. They should be switched on only when an aircraft is heard in order to conserve the aircraft batteries. A vertical beam should not be used as this is not visible in certain conditions. An intermittent beam should be used in preference to a steady one. Aldis lamps may be similarly used.

(*f*) Use your signal cartridges sparingly. They should be used only at night when a aircraft is heard, or in reply to those fired by searching aircraft. Tracer ammunition and smoke bombs have also proved to be useful emergency signalling aids. Remember to keep all pyrotechnics dry and ready for instant use.

(*g*) At a safe distance from the aircraft, and on high ground if possible, lay three fires at least 100 feet apart in the form of a triangle. These may be kept burning continuously if adequate fuel is available, or prepared for use immediately an aircraft is heard or sighted. Use flame by night (burning petrol and oil in sand), and dense smoke by day—adding rubber (parachute cushions, electrical insulation, floor mats, etc.), or urine to produce steam.

Allocation of Duties

51. An allocation of duties, to be carried out when climatic conditions permit, is essential for the morale of the crew, helping to prevent those mental disturbances which are likely to arise in such situations and which are sometimes indicated by out-bursts of temper or moroseness, as well as increasing the chances of rescue.

52. The captain may have to show firmness to ensure that the duties detailed by him are carried out, owing to a natural tendency to let discipline relax.

53. Among the duties allotted by the captain should be that of lookout or aircraft spotter. This is necessary to overcome the necessity of the whole crew being on the alert during the heat of the day. The lookout should have the various signalling devices readily available, and be positioned on the highest ground in the vicinity and near any signal fires that may have

been prepared so that there will be no delay in lighting them when an aircraft is heard or sighted. This duty should be limited to periods of one hour during the heat of the day.

54. The duty of issuing rations is solely that of the captain.

Log Keeping

55. A log should be started as soon as possible and kept throughout the whole period. The first entry should include all details of the emergency: nature of emergency; action taken; date, time, and position of landing or bale-out; names of crew and injuries sustained; weather conditions; equipment and rations available. Subsequent entries should contain details of rations issued, duties allotted, weather, crew morale and physical condition, aircraft sighted, and particulars of any preparations made.

56. The log need not necessarily be kept by the captain, provided he ensures that the correct entries are made. The duty could be delegated to the weakest member of the party, or possibly to an injured man, thereby helping him to overcome a possible feeling that he is a liability on the other survivors.

Preparation of Landing Strip or Dropping Zone

57. The possibility of preparing a suitable stretch of ground nearby for use as an emergency landing strip by rescue aircraft should not be overlooked. Obstructions should be removed and the area clearly marked by strips torn from parachutes. A landing T and the signal $\triangle$ "Probably safe to land here", from the Ground/Air Emergency Code, should be prominently displayed.

58. A dropping zone for supplies should also be clearly indicated on a site adjacent to the camp to prevent them being dropped some distance away. The retrieving of supplies over any distance may well be a task beyond the capabilities of weakened survivors.

WATER
The Importance of Water

59. Water is the key to survival in the desert. Your life expectancy under emergency conditions is determined by the amount

of water available and also the degree to which you can protect your body from direct exposure to the sun and heat, thereby minimising bodily water loss through perspiration and evaporation.

60. The following desert water table shows the number of days of expected survival under two conditions: first, resting in the shade at all times, and second, walking at night and resting by day. It also shows the distances that can be covered.

DESERT WATER TABLE

Days of Expected Survival

Condition	Max. Daily Shade Temp. °F.	Total Available Water per Man (Quarts)					
		0	1	2	4	10	20
Resting in the shade at all times.	120	2½	2½	2½	3	3½	5½
	110	3½	3½	4	4½	6	8½
	100	6	6½	7	8½	11½	16
	90	8½	9½	10½	12½	18	27½
	80	10½	12	13	15½	23	35
	70	12	13	14½	17	24½	38½
	60	12	13	14½	17	25	38½
	50	12	13	14½	17½	25	38½

Condition	Max. Daily Shade Temp. °F.		1	2	4	10
Walking only at night and resting in the shade by day. (Total mileage shown in brackets)	120	1 (25)	2½(25)	2½ (30)	3 (35)	3½ (40)
	110	2½(25)	2½(25)	3 (30)	3½ (35)	4 (40)
	100	3½(25)	4 (25)	4 (30)	5½ (35)	6½ (50)
	90	6 (35)	6½(35)	6½ (40)	8 (55)	9½ (60)
	80	8½(50)	9 (55)	9½ (60)	11½ (70)	14 (90)
	70	9 (55)	9½(60)	11 (80)	12½(102)	16 (130)
	60	9½(60)	10 (70)	11 (100)	13 (130)	17 (180)
	50	9½(70)	10 (90)	11 (120)	13 (180)	17 (180)

61. It will be seen from the table that absence or shortage of water, especially in the higher temperature ranges, severely limits the time of survival or distance travelled. Survival time is not appreciably increased until the available water per man is about four quarts.

Physiological Considerations

62. Water constitutes about 70 per cent. of body weight, so that, as the weight of the average man is about 154 lbs., the human body contains roughly 11 gallons of fluid. Only a maximum of $2\frac{1}{2}$ gallons, or one-fifth, of this can be lost if the individual is to survive. The signs and symptoms of such dehydration are: 1 to 5 per cent. of body fluid lost (up to 4 pints)—thirst, vague discomfort, lack of appetite, flushed skin, impatience, sleepiness and sickness; 6 to 10 per cent. (5 to 9 pints)—dizziness, headache, laboured breathing, absence of salivation, indistinct speech and inability to walk; 11 to 20 per cent. (10 to 18 pints)—delirium, swollen tongue, inability to swallow, deafness, dim vision, numb and shrivelled skin. In the latter stages it will be noted that there is gross muscular weakness and mental capacity may be severely impaired, hence the importance of formulating your plan of action as early as possible and not deviating from it later.

63. It is obvious that, as far as possible, fluid loss should not be permitted to exceed about 8 pints if the survivor is to be kept in reasonably good condition.

64. The ideal use of water under desert survival conditions is to allow a slight negative balance (*e.g.* 3 to 4 pints) to accumulate, and then drink at the rate at which sweating is taking place. In this way there is little impairment in efficiency and no water will be wasted. When the available water supply is reduced to about a pint, this last pint may be used for wetting the mouth, but under hot desert conditions it will have little influence on the duration of survival. The estimation of a negative balance is difficult, but *a moderately severe sensation of thirst is a good indication.* For this reason some pamphlets have advised that no water should be taken during the first 24 hours. While this is good advice for survival at sea under most conditions and under moderate conditions on land, it could be dangerous if the temperature is very high or some work has to be undertaken, as it is quite possible to lose as much as $2\frac{1}{2}$ gallons in that period by sweating.

65. *Individual minimum water requirements therefore depend on loss of water.* This water loss takes place in two ways: by evaporation through sweat, etc., and through the kidneys as urine. Both these losses consist of two parts; a small, steady amount of about 1½ pints per day; and a variable amount, which in the case of the urine is the excess of intake over output (or overflowing of the body "reservoir"), and in the case of evaporation is proportional to the degree of activity of the individual and to the temperature.

66. An indication of the latter loss is that if the daily mean temperature exceeds 80 deg. F., walking at night instead of resting at all times increases the water requirement by 3½ pints per 24 hours. Alternatively, an increase of daily mean temperature from 70 deg. F. to 93 deg. F., under resting conditions, increases the daily water requirement from 1¾ pints to 7 pints. While there are individual variations, in general, sweat loss is proportional to body weight and extreme variations are uncommon.

67. It is often stated that reduction in fluid intake will cause a reduction in the sweat rate. This has been shown to be without foundation. However, if more fluid is taken than is being lost by sweating, the excess will be excreted in the urine and thus lost to the individual.

68. Having obtained a slight degree of dehydration by the method previously outlined, the water should be rationed to the amount estimated to be lost by sweating under the existing conditions, taking into account the mean temperature and activity. When adequate water is available, there is no point in reducing the intake below the amounts shown in para. 69. Smaller amounts will only lead to progressive dehydration and loss of physical and mental efficiency.

69. The following figures are only approximate and assume rest in the shade at all times. In the desert the mean temperature can be taken as 15° F. below the daily maximum.

DAILY WATER REQUIREMENTS TO MAINTAIN WATER BALANCE

Mean Temp. deg. F.	Pints per 24 hrs.
95	9
90	6½
85	4½
80	2½
75	2

At a mean temperature of 65° F. or below (Temperate or Winter Desert Conditions) water loss is at the basal amount of 1¾ pints per 24 hours.

Average summer conditions in and near the Suez Canal Zone are represented by the 90° F. figure.

70. As these figures are for resting in the shade at all times, they are minimum requirements and under survival conditions will often be exceeded, so that an intake of this amount may not be enough to maintain water balance. If the available water supply is insufficient to maintain even the required minimum intake, then a progressive dehydration will take place. Other influencing factors will be the degree of protection that can be obtained from the sun and heat, and the individual activity.

71. Bearing in mind that the sweat loss when walking in the desert in a temperature of just over 100° F. is 2 pints per hour, it will be evident that there is not much future in trying to walk away from a forced landing when the sun is up during the summer. During the winter, of course, considerable distances may be covered.

72. Rationing of water is valuable for morale and to ensure that everyone gets a fair share, but it should not be more severe than indicated in para. 69 if the supplies are available. There is no point in drinking at any particular time and water should be taken at suitable intervals throughout the day. *It is a fallacy that water taken during the heat of the day is immediately lost due to an increase in sweat rate.*

73. Smoking will not increase your actual bodily need for water, but should not be encouraged as it will only lead to an uncomfortable dryness of the mouth. Chewing gum or sucking pebbles may help temporarily to relieve any such dryness, but they are not a substitute for water and will not help in maintaining the level of your body fluid.

74. It can now be seen that just as important as the rationing of water is the rationing of sweat. Keep in the shade at all times during the heat of the day. Work only at night. Keep your body and head well covered, not only as protection against the sun but also to minimize the evaporation of sweat, thereby gaining maximum cooling effect. This covering must be as light and as loose as possible so as to provide adequate ventilation, otherwise an increase in sweat rate will result.

Sources of Water

75. The possibility of replenishing your water supply should not be overlooked. This will largely depend on your location and the season of the year, but do not rely too much on finding water when determining the duration of your stay or travel. The only safe way is to carry with you the water that you need.

76. The following are some of the possible sources of water in desert regions:—

(a) *Wells and Water Holes.* Ensure that these are marked on your map beforehand. They are usually to be found along the caravan routes. As they may be quite deep, with the water level below easy reach, it is advisable to carry a length of light line for lowering a can or some suitable container. The small water holes in dry stream courses, or in other low places known to the natives, are often kept covered with a flat rock or sand and require a careful search for their location. Edges of ancient water holes are built up above their surroundings by accumulations of excrement around them. Look for these mounds.

(b) *Rain.* During the rainy season, rain traps should be erected to catch as much water as possible. Any piece of tarpaulin or dinghy apron can be suspended between four stakes, allowing the water to drain down and accumulate in the centre. An inflated dinghy will also serve this purpose.

(c) *Condensation.* During the cooler months some deserts are humid enough at night for dew to form. To collect this, scoop a shallow basin in the ground and line it with canvas, dinghy apron, or parachute. Over this, pile stones until the basin is filled. During the night the dew will collect on the stones and trickle down on to the lining. Metal parts of the aircraft will also collect dew. Engine cowlings should be removed and placed upside down to allow the moisture to accumulate. Dew should be collected at first light before evaporation takes place.

(d) *Dry Stream Beds and Gullies.* By digging at the lowest point of the outside of a bend in the bed of a channel, or the lowest point between dunes, a source of water may be found. If wet sand or mud is found, put it in a cloth and wring out the water.

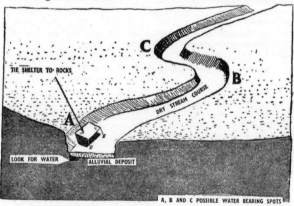

TIE SHELTER TO ROCKS.

A

LOOK FOR WATER   ALLUVIAL DEPOSIT

C

DRY STREAM COURSE

B

A, B AND C POSSIBLE WATER BEARING SPOTS

WATER AND SHELTER IN A DRY STREAM COURSE

(e) *Sandy Beaches.* The water first revealed by digging a hole just above the high-tide mark should be fit for drinking. Further digging only produces water which is too salty.

26

(*f*) *Desert Plants.* Some desert plants store water in their trunks, branches or roots. Such plants are found mainly along desert fringes in semi-arid terrain and near water holes. Avoid plants with milky sap—they are poisonous. The presence of vegetation is not always a sign that water is available. In the Middle East, for example, the palm is the only plant which indicates that water is close at hand.

Purification of Water

77. Water obtained by any of the methods previously outlined, or tinned water that may be tainted or suspect, should be purified before drinking by one of the following methods:—

(*a*) *Halazone Tablets.* Crush and dissolve one halazone tablet in each pint of water. Shake well and allow to stand one hour before drinking. If this is insufficient to produce a distinct smell of chlorine, add more tablets until the odour is present.

(*b*) *Boiling.* Boil the water for at least three minutes and allow any sediment to settle while cooling.

(*c*) *Iodine.* Add two or three drops of iodine to each quart of water and allow to stand for 30 minutes.

DONT DRINK UNPURIFIED WATER—it will only lead to dysentery.

DON'T DRINK ALCOHOL—it will cause nausea and increase thirst. It is dangerous to drink alcohol under such conditions and may even bring about convulsions.

DON'T DRINK URINE—it is poisonous and will decrease your resistance and increase your thirst.

SALT

78. Sweat contains salt as well as water, and the loss of this salt must be made good, otherwise you may suffer from heatstroke, heat exhaustion, or muscular cramps.

79. One of the ways in which a man gets used to hot climates is by replenishing the amount of salt lost in the sweat. This is particularly necessary during the first week, when maximum sweating is likely to occur.

80. Under normal living conditions enough extra salt can be absorbed with the food at mealtimes, but under survival conditions two or three salt tablets should be taken every day provided that an adequate supply of water is available.

FOOD

81. There is little animal or plant life in the true desert regions and you should never rely on replenishing your food supplies from these sources. When you reach an oasis you are no longer in the desert in the survival sense, for you have reached a populated area and your rescue is only a matter of time. However, food is less important than water. You can manage without food for several days with no ill effects.

82. Food spoils quickly in the desert. Tinned emergency rations should be opened only as needed and the contents eaten as soon as possible after the containers have been opened.

Animal Food

83. The presence of game animals depends primarily on the presence of water and cover, and there is little of either in the true desert. Look for animals at water holes, in low-lying areas where there is a greater chance of moisture, under rocks, and in bushes. They are more commonly seen at dusk or dawn than during the heat of the day. The most common animals are small rodents (rabbits, desert dogs, rats) and lizards. Rodents may be caught by finding their burrows and snaring them with a loop snare when they come out at dusk or dawn. Gazelles or antelopes may be found in the open desert and may be taken by a good shot with a rifle, but don't go chasing them or you may wander too far and become lost, or at least expend precious energy and water, all to no avail.

84. Animal food will be difficult to find in the Middle Eastern deserts, but in the Gobi herds of antelope numbering up to a hundred animals may be encountered: on the other hand you may strike areas where there are none at all. The most common forms of animal life in the deserts of Iran and Iraq are birds, such as partridge, quail, and bustard, which frequent the river beds and other water sources.

Plant Food

85. Edible plant food is rare in the desert. Grasses are edible, as are some of the wild plants or their roots that may be found along dry stream beds or around water holes, but they are unlikely to be palatable or possess any real nutritive value. If you are tempted to try any plant food, avoid those with a milky or coloured sap—they are poisonous—and eat only a small quantity. Wait eight hours and if there are no ill effects, such as vomiting or diarrhoea, repeat the dose and wait for a similar period. If there are still no ill effects, you can eat reasonable quantities with safety.

86. Palms, which are found near water holes, will provide food in the form of dates and the palm cabbage, a tender shoot which extends up from the top of the trunk at the point where the leaves spread out. It may be eaten raw or cooked.

CLOTHING

DESERT CLOTHING

87. Clothing is of the greatest importance in the maintenance of health in hot climates, as a protection against the sun, heat, thorns, and insect bites. It protects the body against excessive loss of fluid and salts by sweating, so that if you go around without a shirt much of the sweat may evaporate quickly without your notice. Keep your body and head covered during the heat of the day, otherwise you will very likely suffer from sunburn, heatstroke, or heat exhaustion.

Body

88. Light, loose-fitting clothes are best. The air space between the loose garment and the body acts as an insulator against the

heat of the sun. The natives have discovered this fact by experience and have adopted loose flowing robes. Sleeves should be kept loose and flapping. The legs should also be kept covered, and slacks worn in preference to shorts.

89. The stomach should be carefully protected both day and night. It is particularly susceptible to chill resulting from the drop in temperature at night, or to cooling by the evaporation of sweat. Such chilling may lead to acute diarrhoea or even dysentery. Do not sleep with the stomach uncovered: an improvised woollen band worn round the waist at all times will guard against this rapid chilling.

90. Owing to the extremes in temperature, the need for additional clothing will be felt at night. If warm clothing is not available, use your parachute to make a sleeping bag, wrapping several thicknesses round yourself cocoon fashion.

Head

91. It is particularly important to protect the head and back of the neck against direct exposure to the sun. A service cap provides safe protection against sunstroke, provided a piece of cloth is hung over the back of the head, neck, and shoulders.

CUT

HEADGEAR FASHIONED
FROM SEAT CUSHION

92. If you have no hat, protection can be obtained by improvising a seat cushion. The cushion should be slit open, and a piece of shroud line used as a chin strap to secure it on the head.

93. An alternative form of headgear, and one more suitable in hot climates, can be copied from the Arab headdress as follows:—

(*a*) Make a 4-foot square composed of several layers of parachute cloth.

(*b*) Make a double rope loop about the size of the crown of your head (size of hat band).

(*c*) Put a wadded handkerchief or cloth on top of your head. Fold the square of cloth diagonally and place it on top of the handkerchief; fasten in place by the loop of rope.

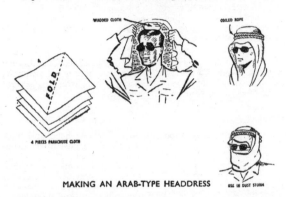

MAKING AN ARAB-TYPE HEADDRESS

94. This headdress has the additional advantage of affording protection for the face against swirling sand during sandstorms, when the tails of the covering can be tucked across the face. Failing this, an improvised face cloth should be tied over the lower part of the face.

Eyes.

95. Eyes must be protected against glare, both direct and reflected. Sun glasses or dark goggles must be worn throughout the day. Goggles have the advantage of protecting the eyes during sandstorms, but unless they are adequately ventilated may prove uncomfortable during the heat of the day.

96. If neither glasses nor **goggles** are available, a piece of cloth with slits cut for the eyes (just large enough to allow a penny to pass through) makes a good eyeshield. Smearing soot under the eyes helps to reduce glare.

CUT NARROW SLITS IN PIECE OF CLOTH FOR IMPROVISED EYESHIELDS

Feet

97. The feet should be kept in good condition. This is very important, as on it may depend your return to safety. They should be inspected at frequent intervals and shoes should be removed when resting and emptied of sand.

98. Socks should be changed regularly. If you can wear two pairs of socks, the inside pair should be worn inside-out and the two pairs should be interchanged at intervals.

99. Thin soles can be reinforced by lacing on an outer sole improvised from rubber floor covering or tyre walls.

100. Unless you are wearing flying boots, you must try to prevent sand entering your shoes. Make a pair of puttees from strips of parachute cloth, covering an inch or two of the shoe tops and three inches of the legs. Slacks should be worn outside the puttees to maintain adequate air circulation.

PUTTEES OF PARACHUTE CLOTH WILL KEEP SAND AND INSECTS OUT OF SHOES

101. If you lose your shoes, or if they wear out, improvise a practical pair of sandals using floor covering or the rubber side-wall of a tyre for the soles and parachute cloth or canvas for the uppers and heel straps. The felt covering of the T3180, "Walter" Transmitter, will provide a comfortable inner sole.

IMPROVISED SANDAL

General

102. If you are caught out in a sandstorm, button up your clothing tightly, fastening wrist bands and trouser bottoms. Cover the face with a cloth and lie down, back to wind. To avoid sand piling up around you, roll about from time to time.

103. Always inspect clothing carefully and shake it thoroughly before putting it on, to guard against spiders and scorpions.

FIREMAKING

104. Fires will be needed for warmth at night, especially during the winter months, and for signalling, cooking, and purifying water by boiling. A hot drink, even if it is only water, is a great morale raiser.

105. Provided oil and petrol are available from the aircraft, the problem of firemaking is simple. You can make a stove out of any metal container or by building stones in a small circle. Fill the container with sand drenched with oil, then add a little petrol and light with a match. Holes should be made at the

IMPROVISED STOVE USING PETROL

33

lower end to allow ventilation and round the top to let the flame and smoke out. Try to wall your fire in to concentrate the heat and provide a platform for your cooking pot. Never add petrol to a fire already started or even smouldering.

106. Lubricating oil will not burn directly, but you can use it for fuel with a wick arrangement. The wick can be made of rope, string, rag, or even a cigarette.

IMPROVISED STOVE TO BURN
OIL AND ANIMAL FAT

107. In and near oases, stems of palm leaves and similar wood will serve as fuel. Out in the open desert, use scrub or any dead vegetation. Dry roots will burn well—a small stick protruding out of the sand will often yield enough fuel to boil a can of water if the roots are dug out carefully.

108. Dried camel dung makes a good emergency fuel, burning with a smoky yellow flame.

109. Conserve your matches. Try to light a fire with just one match. If using a wood or scrub fire, always start in a small way and build up your fire gradually. Use small pieces of wood arranged in a low pyramid, with lint from unravelled cloth, rope, or first aid gauze bandage to start the fire. A few drops of petrol will make this kind of tinder catch very readily.

110. Fires can also be kindled without using matches. The flint and steel is one method, especially when petrol is available. A lens from a camera, binoculars, or reflector sight, can be used in bright sunlight to concentrate the sun's rays on tinder and start it burning. If the aircraft battery is serviceable, a spark can be produced by scratching together the bare ends of two wires connected to the battery.

111. Always build your fire on the leeward side of the aircraft or shelter.

NATIVES

112. In desert areas most habitations are along the coastal strips or near the water holes and oases. In most deserts there are also wandering tribes, following the trails and caravan routes from water hole to water hole.

113. Learn as much as possible about the natives in the area in which you have to operate. Study their habits, religious customs and manners—it may be of use to you some day. They are usually a proud and independent people, with a way of life and a culture that they value highly. Their habits may appear peculiar to you, but do not scoff at them. Remember that to them *you* are the strange ones. Be especially careful not to offend them.

114. With few exceptions natives are friendly. They know the country, its trails, food and water sources, and can be the means of your being speedily returned to civilization. In short, they are your best help—but it all depends on how you approach them.

115. Hostile parties may be encountered in certain areas (*e.g.* Southern Arabia). Be on your guard against them. If you do meet this type of native, then "blood chits", money and great tact may see you through.

116. When dealing with natives the following rules should be observed:—

(*a*) Don't rush matters. They may be shy and unapproachable at first. Show courtesy and patience. A gift and a friendly manner will help to open negotiations.

(*b*) Always deal with the recognized headman or chief.

(*c*) Ask for help—don't demand it.

(*d*) If you make a promise, keep it.

(*e*) Respect personal property. Always make some kind of payment for what you receive.

35

(*f*) Avoid things that are taboo, such as native women, certain animals, etc.

(*g*) Leave a good impression. Other crews may need their help later and you can go a long way to making things easier for them by your manner and appreciation of hospitality and help.

ALWAYS BE TACTFUL, PATIENT, AND HONEST.

DESERT AILMENTS

117. Protection of health is of the first importance under survival conditions. Whether you stay with the aircraft or decide to walk out, your physical condition will have a lot to do with your coming out safely.

118. The following are the chief desert illnesses. With the exception of the last, all are attributable to excessive exposure to sun and heat and can be guarded against by keeping the body and head protected and by remaining in the shade during the heat of the day.

(*a*) *Heat Cramps.* Usually the first warning of heat exhaustion. The cramps usually occur in the muscles which are actually in use, probably the abdomen, arms, and legs. Caused by lack of body salt after a person has been sweating a great deal, especially if extra salt has not been taken. Symptoms are shallow breathing, vomiting, and dizziness. Treatment is to move the person into the shade and give salt dissolved in water (two tablets to a quart) until the cramps are relieved.

(*b*) *Heat Exhaustion.* Caused by exposure to high temperature and humidity, resulting in loss of body fluids through excessive sweating. May occur without direct exposure to the sun. The face is pale and the skin cold and sweating. Accompanied by nausea, dizziness, weakness, and perhaps cramps. The pulse is weak and the person may become delirious or unconcious. Treat as for heat cramps and keep the person at rest.

(c) **Heatstroke.** The third and most serious result of over-exposure to the direct rays of the sun, although it can affect a person who has been under cover. Symptoms are a hot, dry skin; sweating stops; the face is flushed and feverish; temperature rises and the pulse rate becomes fast and strong; there is severe headache and often vomiting. Unconsciousness may follow. Treatment is to lower the body temperature as soon as possible. Lay the person in the shade, with head and shoulders slightly raised. Remove outer clothing and cool the body by wetting the underclothing with water and by fanning. If water for cooling is not available, scoop out a trench in the sand and place the person in the bottom. Rig a sun awning, leaving an air space for ventilation. As soon as consciousness returns, give water with salt tablets added (two tablets to a quart). When the temperature is back to normal, replace clothing and keep warm to prevent a chill.

(d) **Sunburn.** A very painful and unnecessary ailment caused by excessive exposure of the body to the sun, particularly when not acclimatized. It can be dangerous: if more than two-thirds of the body is affected, sunburn is likely to prove fatal. Treat affected parts with sunburn cream.

(e) **Sore Eyes.** Excessive exposure of unprotected eyes to direct sunlight, glare, or dust particles, will result in them becoming sore. Treat with boracic ointment and bandage lightly. In the absence of a suitable ointment a damp bandage should be applied.

(f) **Constipation or Difficult Urination.** Can be expected with a shortage of food and water and should not give cause for alarm. Indiscriminate use of laxative tablets will also lead to an increase in urine, with consequent loss of body fluid and salt.

119. Desert sores may develop when the skin is broken under survival conditions. All wounds, however trivial, should be promptly treated with antiseptic ointment, if available, and covered with a sterile bandage.

120. If it is decided that the chances of rescue from the crash position are remote and the only hope of survival is to walk out, then careful plans must be made before setting out on what may well be a journey of considerable duration. A desert trek is not to be embarked on lightly, and should be undertaken only if it is certain that the objective can be reached on the water supply available. Do not underestimate the difficulties that will be encountered or overestimate your physical condition.

121. It may not be advisable for the entire crew to attempt the journey ; it may be better for say two members to set out for help, the remainder awaiting rescue with the aircraft. This will depend on the situation and the supplies available, especially water. One advantage of this method is that you have a double chance of coming through.

Preparations for Travel

122. Check all available equipment and decide which items to take with you. Don't overload—the total weight of equipment carried by each person should not exceed 35 lbs. As water will be your chief requirement, it should comprise the greater part of this weight allowance (1 Gallon=10 lbs.); the remainder should consist of signalling equipment and some material from which you can improvise a shelter, preferably a piece of parachute canopy. Other smaller necessities are a compass, maps, pencil and paper, knife, salt and halazone tablets, sunglasses, first aid kit, torch, and of course a watch. A bare minimum of food should be taken, especially if you are short of water. It may be possible to improvise a walking stick from some part of the aircraft structure.

123. A good rucksack can easily be made from a seat-type parachute by trimming it and cutting off the excess harness and back pad. Other types of parachute packs can be modified in this way with a little thought and ingenuity.

124. A lighter, but less comfortable, pack can be made by simply wrapping the equipment in the canopy and securing it by the harness straps or rigging lines. Always try to make the pack sit as high as possible on the shoulders so that it will not bang in the small of the back at every step.

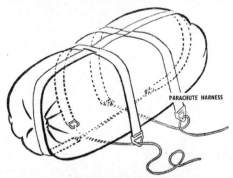

PARACHUTE HARNESS

IMPROVISED ROLL-TYPE PACK

125. Before leaving the aircraft, destroy all classified documents and any secret equipment. Leave a note in a prominent position, detailing the members of the party, direction in which travelling and objective, and the date set out. Your route should be marked if possible, and a log and sketch map maintained.

Hints on Travel

126. During the hottest part of the year travel should be undertaken only at night, although considerable distances may be covered in daylight in the winter months. A double awning should be made with a parachute canopy to provide shade during the heat of the day. Rest in the shade at all times and get as much sleep as possible. Remove shoes and socks when resting.

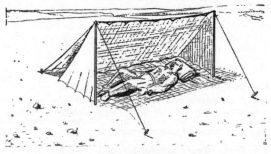

LIGHT SHELTER

127. Don't hurry. Adjust your pace to that of the slowest man and use a long, slow gait rather than short, quick steps. Follow the easiest route and avoid soft sand areas and rough terrain as much as possible. A good idea is to make a compulsory halt for ten minutes every hour. Shoes should be emptied of sand at frequent intervals.

128. When marching at night, map reading and pinpointing may not be easy. Even on clear nights there is a lack of perspective which can have serious consequences. A drop of fifty or sixty feet may appear to be only a slight dip. A torch in these circumstances is a necessity, and it is advisable for the party to walk in single file.

Choosing the Route

129. Your position should be accurately determined and marked on the map before setting out. When deciding your objective, it is better to choose one that is easy to find—*e.g.* a coast or road which can then be followed until habitation is reached—rather than a specific objective such as a settlement or oasis. In this

way you can allow for a greater margin of error in your direction. If a definite objective is decided upon, note any prominent adjoining feature, perhaps a road leading to it or a range of hills, to help you in locating it.

130. If you have come down in an area in which there are trails, these will lead you to water. Follow the arrow-head formed by converging trails to reach the nearest water hole.

131. Once you have decided on your objective, *stick to it.*

How to Determine and Maintain Direction

132. A compass is provided in the survival pack to enable you to determine direction. If this is not available, use the compass from the aircraft but remember to remove the compensating magnets. Allow for magnetic variation as shown on your maps.

133. Even without a compass it is possible to determine direction. If your objective is a large one, such as a coast-line, the simple fact that the sun rises in the east and sets in the west should be sufficient indication of your direction of travel. Actually the sun rises due east and sets due west only on March 21st and September 23rd—the equinoxes. If you wish to estimate the point of sunrise with greater accuracy, the following table will give you the angle of sunrise from true north at different times of the year and at different latitudes.

SUNRISE TABLE

DIRECTION IN WHICH SUN RISES — DEGREES EAST OF TRUE NORTH
Direction measured when top of sun just shows above horizon.

LATITUDE	MAR. 21	MAY 5	JUNE 22	AUG. 9	SEPT. 23	NOV. 7	DEC. 22	FEB. 5
60° North	89°	55°	37°	55°	89°	122°	140°	122°
30° North	90°	71°	63°	71°	90°	108°	116°	108°
0° (Equator)	90°	74°	67°	74°	90°	106°	113°	106°
30° South	90°	72°	64°	72°	90°	104°	117°	109°

134. **Geographic** north and south may be found by the shadow cast by the sun. If you have the correct local time on your watch, the shadow cast by an object at 1200 hours will indicate north and south. The object must be straight and perpendicular to the ground. In the northern hemisphere the base of the shadow will indicate south and the tip of the shadow will indicate north. If you have no watch you may still obtain direction by the shadow cast by the sun. Place a stick or other straight object in the ground on a level spot. Starting in the morning and continuing throughout the day, about once every hour, mark the point at the tip of the shadow. At the end connect these points and you will have a line running true east and west. A perpendicular to this line will indicate north and south.

135. By night, if the sky is clear, true north and south can be determined by the stars. In the northern hemisphere, true north can be ascertained from the constellation of the Great Bear, which points to Polaris (North Star). In the southern hemisphere, the Southern Cross indicates true south.

136. Once course has been set, direction should be maintained by compass. If you have no compass, pick two easily visible objects which are exactly on the line you want to follow and as far apart as possible, and keep them in line while walking. Before reaching the first object, pick a third landmark in the same line ahead and repeat the process. This method is not always reliable or feasible in featureless country, such as that encountered in most deserts.

137. When resting, face in the direction of travel or make a pointer on the ground so that when you resume the march you are certain of travelling in the same direction.

How to Determine Distance

138. Distances in the desert can be deceptive. Owing to the clear atmosphere, objects appear to be much closer than they actually are. Visual estimations of distance should be multiplied by three. To keep an accurate check of distance travelled, and to be able to plot this on your map, it is necessary to evolve a more accurate method of determining distance than just by visual estimations.

GREAT BEAR

GREAT BEAR AND NORTH STAR

SOUTHERN CROSS

139. On level, open ground with a good surface, the average individual walks about 2½ miles per hour. With practice, a good estimation of the distance travelled can be made by reference to your watch. Another method that is even more accurate, and probably safer to use in desert travel, is to count the number of paces taken. The natural stride of a man is about 2½ feet (10 feet every 4 steps). A combination of both methods can be used to check the accuracy of one against the other.

How to Plot Direction and Distance

140. A protractor and scale are necessary to plot direction and distance.

141. If a protractor is not available, one can be improvised from a piece of paper as shown in the accompanying diagram. Fold the paper as illustrated. When it is unfolded, the angles formed by the creases should be marked in pencil.

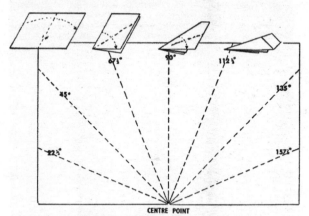

CENTRE POINT

PROTRACTOR MADE BY FOLDING PAPER

45

142. A scale can also be improvised by folding a strip of paper into equal divisions. Mark the creases at the edge of the paper and let each division represent 1,000 feet, or any other convenient interval you choose to plot.

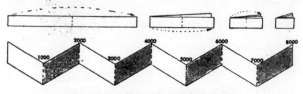

SCALE IMPROVISED FROM FOLDED PAPER

143. If an obstacle should force you to alter the direction of travel, the alteration of course should be determined by compass and the distance by pace counting. This will enable the alteration to be plotted and the new direction and distance estimated to reach the objective or to resume the original line of travel.

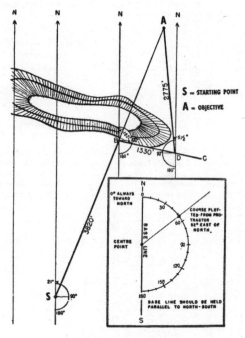

S = STARTING POINT

A = OBJECTIVE

HOW TO PLOT A COURSE

47

Ground/Air Emergency Code for Use in Air/Land Rescue Search

KEY

1 REQUIRE DOCTOR, SERIOUS INJURIES
2 REQUIRE MEDICAL SUPPLIES
3 UNABLE TO PROCEED
4 REQUIRE FOOD AND WATER
5 REQUIRE FIREARMS AND AMMUNITION
6 REQUIRE MAP AND COMPASS
7 REQUIRE SIGNAL LAMP WITH BATTERY, & RADIO
8 INDICATE DIRECTION TO PROCEED
9 AM PROCEEDING IN THIS DIRECTION

10 WILL ATTEMPT TAKE-OFF
11 AIRCRAFT SERIOUSLY DAMAGED
12 PROBABLY SAFE TO LAND HERE
13 REQUIRE FUEL AND OIL
14 ALL WELL
15 NO
16 YES
17 NOT UNDERSTOOD
18 REQUIRE ENGINEER

CODE

1 —	6 □	10 |>
2 — —	7 — ·	11 ⌐|
3 X	8 K	12 △
4 F	9 ←	13 ⌐
5 >>		14 LL
		15 Z
		16 Y
		17 —|>
		18 W

* A SPACE OF 10 FT BETWEEN ELEMENTS WHEREVER POSSIBLE

Notes

Notes

Notes

....
....
....
....
....
....
....
....
....
....
....
....
....
....
....
....
....
....
....

Notes

Notes

Notes

....
....
....
....
....
....
....
....
....
....
....
....
....
....
....
....
....
....
....
....
....

Notes

....
....
....
....
....
....
....
....
....
....
....
....
....
....
....
....
....
....
....
....

Notes

Notes

57

First issued to airmen in the 1950s, this reprint of The Air Ministry's Sea Survival pamphlet includes emergency advice to crew operating over sea regions.

Packed with original line drawings and instruction in:

- How to punch man-eating sharks, which are 'cowards'

- The pros and cons of drinking 'fish juice'

- When to smoke

OUT NOW

First issued to airmen in the 1950s, this reprint of The Air Ministry's Arctic Survival pamphlet includes emergency advice to crew operating over arctic regions.

Packed with original line drawings and instruction in:

- The best faces to pull to prevent frostbite and, should you fail, when you can expect bits of you to 'fall off'

- How to build a structurally sound igloo

- How to fashion a mask to prevent snowblindness

OUT NOW

First issued to airmen in the 1950s, this reprint of The Air Ministry's Jungle Survival pamphlet includes emergency advice to crew operating over jungle regions.

Packed with original line drawings and instruction in:

- What to do if 'jungle hiking becomes boring'

- How to stay safe from poisonous reptiles and insects

- The benefits of using a 'fire thong'

OUT NOW